D1527081

Seventeen Syllables
of Grace

John W. Stevens

ISBN: 9798762476089

DEDICATION

This collection is dedicated to all of the people who have used these prayers daily for the last six years.

You remind me of what God's Grace looks like in the world.

INTRODUCTION

I have an addiction to Grace. You have probably seen the word typed with "g" being in the lower case, such as, "grace." For me, the word has always spoken louder than that, and needed more emphasis. The word Grace needed to be treated as a proper noun.

Grace for me rounds out the Trinity, perhaps becoming in some theological sense the glue that holds the three persons together; moving in, through and around the Creator, the Christ and the Holy Spirit.

Grace is my favorite idea, concept, and theological construct to write, dream, and claim as a gift from the above mentioned three. So, over the last six years of writing Haiku Prayers, Grace has found itself being given front seat in many of them.

This collection, "Seventeen Syllables of Grace," is a celebration of Grace, and a poetic love letter to that which is given freely, claiming and renaming us as Saints. I hope you find these prayers as moving as I found writing them, and I hope that they might find their way into your own prayers.

Living in God's Amazing Grace,

John W. Stevens
November 18th, 2021

You love us all, God,
before we can do a thing.
Made Saints by Your Grace.

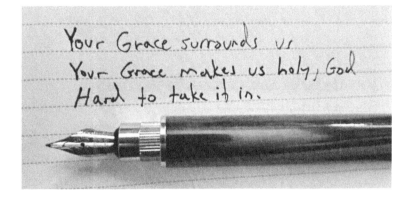

Your Grace surrounds us.
Your Grace makes us holy, God.
Hard to take it in.

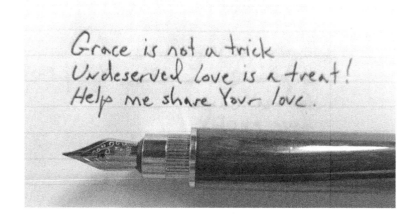

Grace is not a trick.
Undeserved love is a treat!
Help me share Your love.

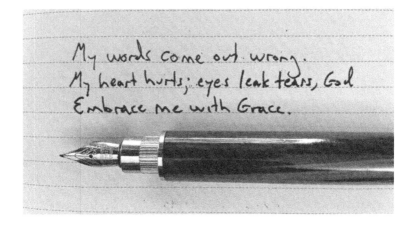

My words come out wrong.
My heart hurts; eyes leak tears, God.
Embrace me with Grace.

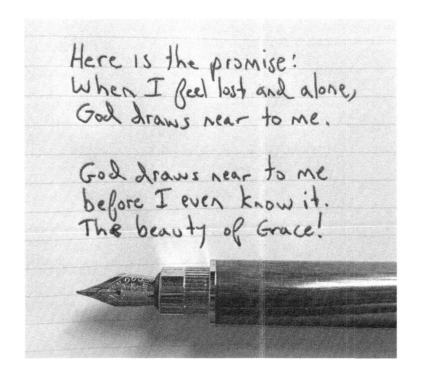

Here is the promise:
When I feel lost and alone,
God draws near to me.

God draws near to me
before I even know it.
The beauty of Grace.

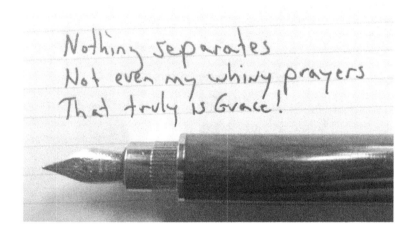

Nothing separates.
Not even my whiny prayers.
That truly is Grace!

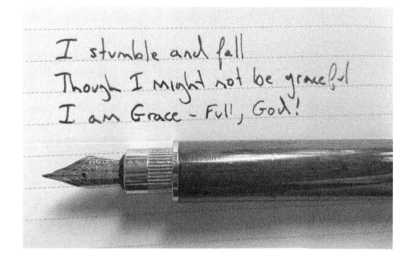

I stumble and fall.
Though I might not be graceful,
I am Grace-Full, God!

I'm afraid I've lost
the game of life and my heart.
Grace makes life point-less

Grace makes life point-less
No longer do we keep score
God's Grace cleans the slate

God's Grace cleans the slate
helping me see Christ's hope when
I'm afraid I've lost.

I'm afraid I've lost
the game of life and my heart.
Grace makes life point-less.

Grace makes life point-less.
No longer do we keep score.
God's Grace cleans the slate.

God's Grace cleans the slate,
helping me see Christ's hope when
I'm afraid I've lost.

I look to th skies
I watch for Christ to come
Head held high with hope

Head held high with hope
I watch for Christ around us
Found in the Stranger

Found in the Stranger
I watch for Christ within us
Found offering Grace!

I look to the skies.
I watch for Christ to come.
Head held high with hope.

Head held high with hope.
I watch for Christ around us,
found in the stranger.

Found in the stranger,
I watch for Christ within us,
found offering Grace!

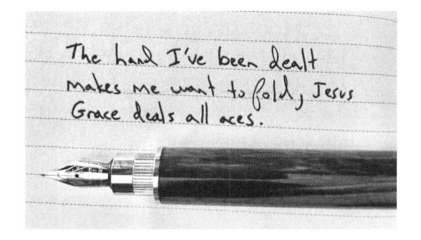

The hand I've been dealt
makes me want to fold, Jesus.
Grace deals all aces.

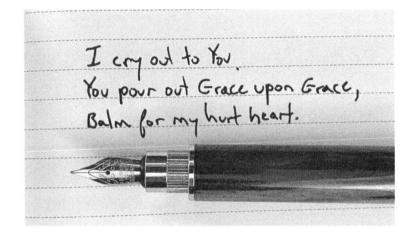

I cry out to You.
You pour out Grace upon Grace;
Balm for my hurt heart.

Do You love me, God?
Help me remember this fact:
Grace claims all of us!

I think silly things.
Like how can I be loved, God?
Grace makes it all so!

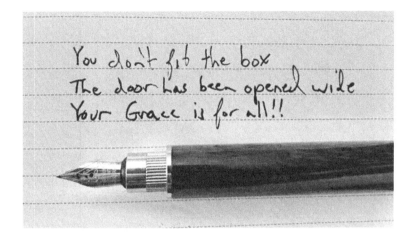

You don't fit the box.
The door has been opened wide.
Your Grace is for all!

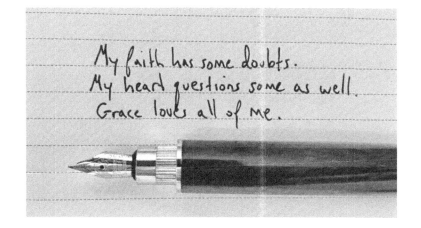

My faith has some doubts.
My heart questions some as well.
Grace loves all of me.

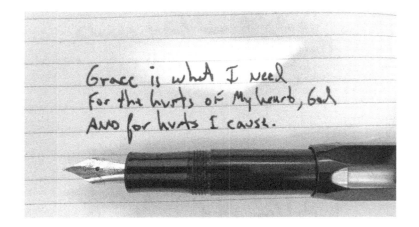

Grace is what I need
for the hurts of my heart, God,
AND for hurts I cause.

My heart needs You, God.
Give me Grace tinted glasses
to help me love more.

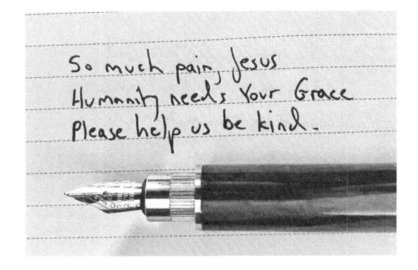

So much pain, Jesus.
Humanity needs Your Grace.
Please help us be kind.

We are all searching.
Please tell us the truth, Jesus.
Grace makes us enough.

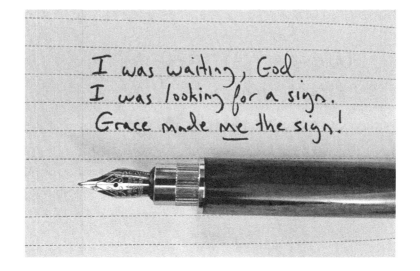

I was waiting, God.
I was looking for a sign.
Grace made <u>me</u> the sign!

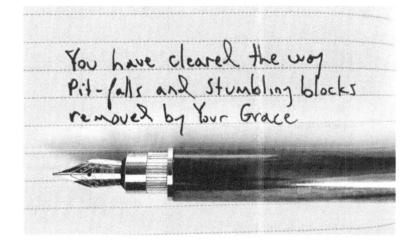

You have cleared the way.
Pit-falls and Stumbling blocks
removed by Your Grace.

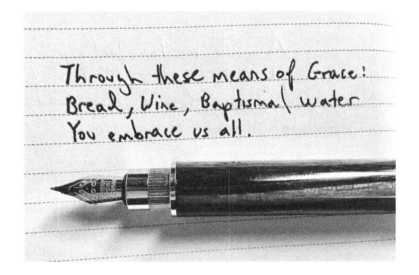

Through these means of Grace:
Bread, Wine, Baptismal Water,
You embrace us all.

Heart has many rooms.
So many places to hide.
Grace finds me, again!

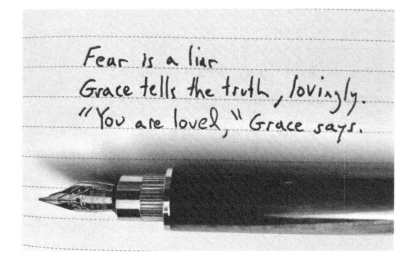

Fear is a liar.
Grace tells the truth, lovingly.
"You are loved," Grace says.

God, You are so weird!
You love me before I act.
Grace is surprising.

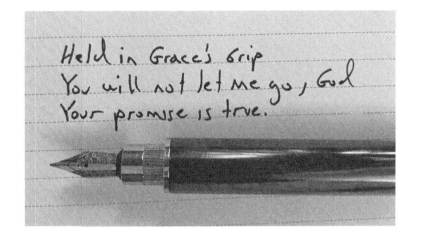

Held in Grace's grip.
You will not let me go, God.
Your promise is true.

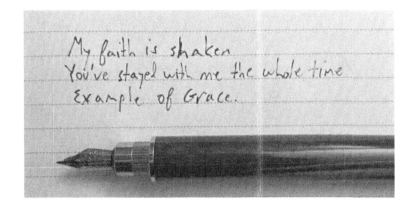

My faith is shaken.
You've stayed with me the whole time.
Example of Grace.

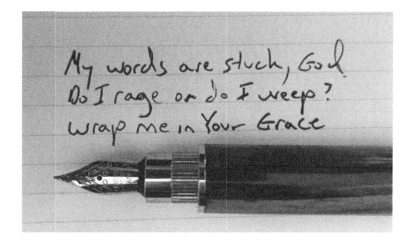

My words are stuck, God.
Do I rage or do I weep?
Wrap me in Your Grace.

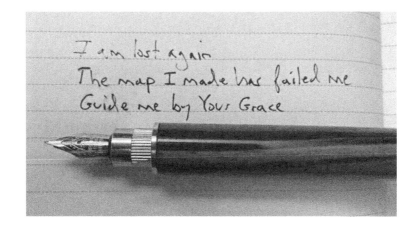

I am lost again.
The map I made has failed me.
Guide me by Your Grace.

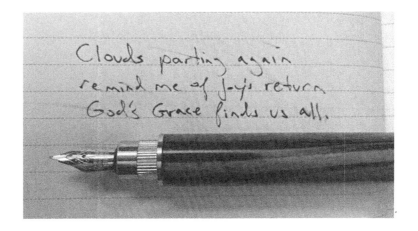

Clouds parting again
remind me of Joy's return.
God's Grace finds us all.

Jesus, I need bread.
Crumbs from Your table of Grace.
You give me new life!

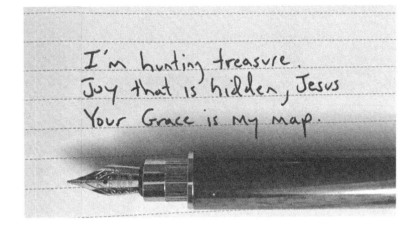

I'm hunting treasure.
Joy that is hidden, Jesus.
Your Grace is my map.

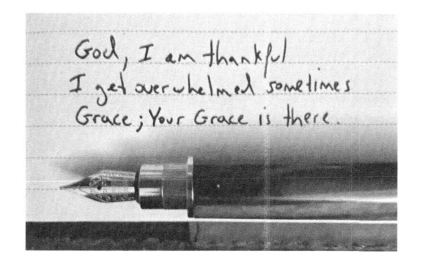

God, I am thankful.
I get overwhelmed sometimes.
Grace; Your Grace is there.

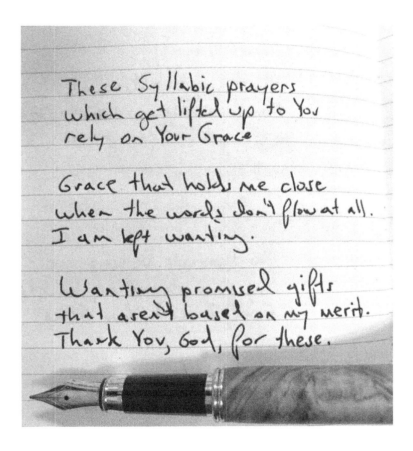

These Syllabic prayers
which get lifted up to You
rely on Your Grace

Grace that holds me close
when the words don't flow at all.
I am left wanting.

Wanting promised gifts
that aren't based on my merit.
Thank You, God, for these.

These syllabic prayers
which get lifted up to You
rely on Your Grace.

Grace that holds me close
when the words don't flow at all.
I am left wanting.

Wanting promised gifts
that aren't based on my merit.
Thank You, God, for these.

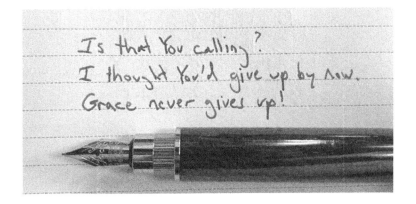

Is that You calling?
I thought You'd give up by now.
Grace never gives up.

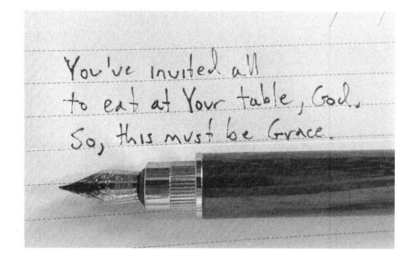

You've invited all
to eat at Your table, God.
So, this must be Grace.

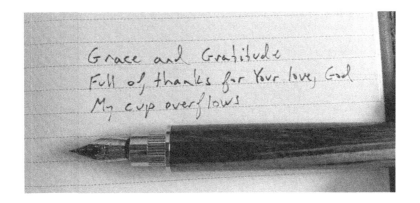

Grace and Gratitude
Full of thanks for Your love, God.
My cup overflows.

I cannot explain
(or understand) Your Grace, God.
Still, I am thankful.

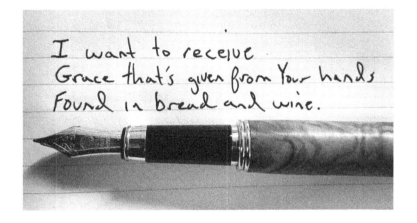

I want to receive
Grace that's given from Your hands
found in bread and wine.

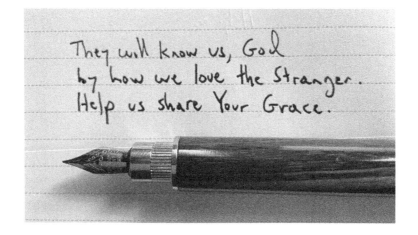

They will know us, God
by how we love the stranger.
Help us share Your Grace.

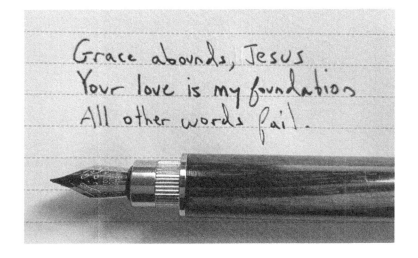

Grace abounds, Jesus.
Your love is my foundation.
All other words fail.

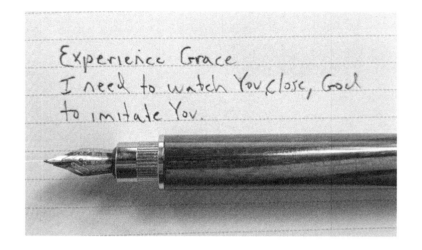

Experience Grace.
I need to watch You close, God,
to imitate You.

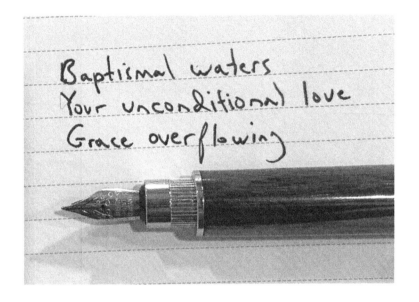

Baptismal waters
Your unconditional love
Grace overflowing

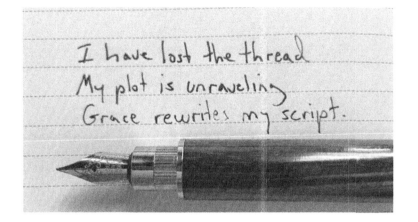

I have lost the thread.
My plot is unraveling.
Grace rewrites my script.

Your Grace has claimed me.
You call me out of hiding.
Bringing me to life.

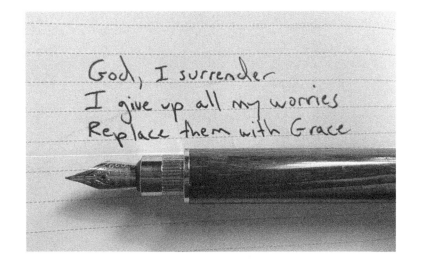

God, I surrender.
I give up all my worries.
Replace them with Grace.

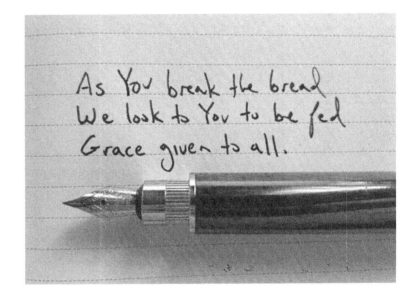

As You break the bread,
we look to You to be fed.
Grace given to all.

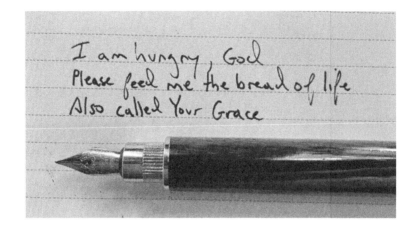

I am hungry, God.
Please feed me the bread of life,
also called Your Grace.

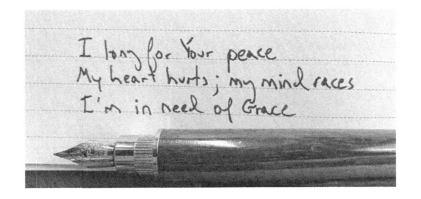

I long for Your peace.
My heart hurts; my mind races.
I'm in need of Grace.

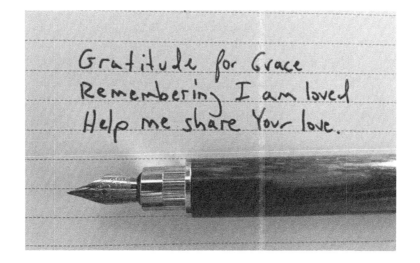

Gratitude for Grace.
Remembering I am loved.
Help me share Your love.

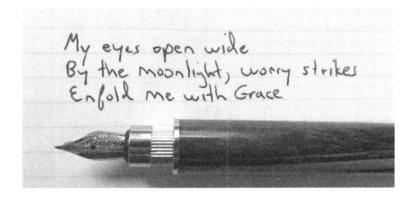

My eyes open wide.
By the moonlight, worry strikes.
Enfold me with Grace.

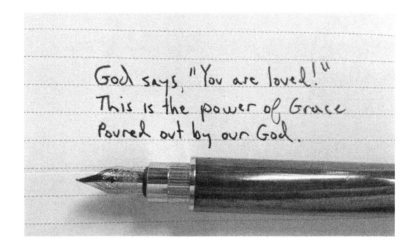

God says, 'You are loved!"
This is the power of Grace
Poured out by our God.

Tape measure busted.
You love me beyond measure!
Measured by Your Grace.

Grace connects us all
extending a cosmic hand
lifting us through love.

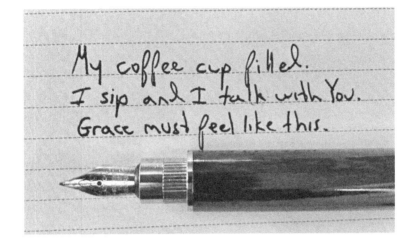

My coffee cup filled.
I sip and I talk with You.
Grace must feel like this.

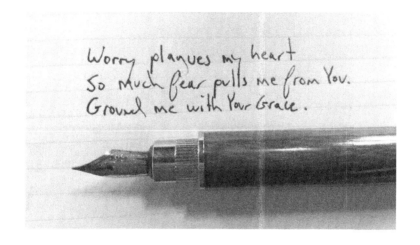

Worry plagues my heart.
So much fear pulls me from You.
Ground me with Your Grace.

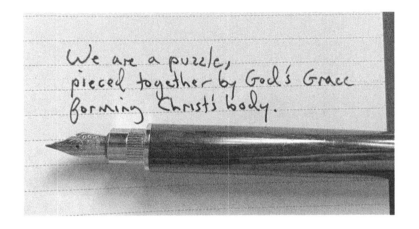

We are a puzzle,
pieced together by God's Grace,
forming Christ's body.

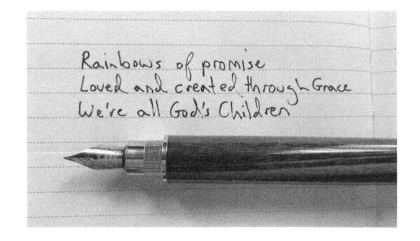

Rainbows of promise.
Loved and created through Grace,
We're all God's Children.

Left hand and these smears
remind me ways I'm unique.
Grace looks like rainbows.

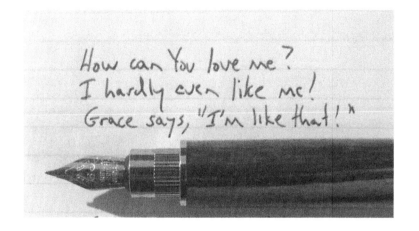

How can You love me?
I hardly even like me!
Grace says, "I'm like that!"

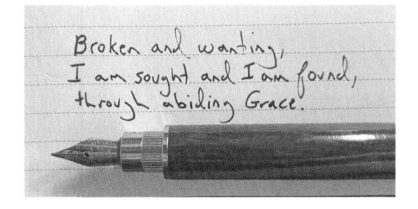

Broken and wanting,
I am sought and I am found,
through abiding Grace.

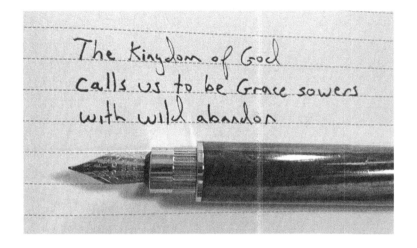

The Kingdom of God
calls us to be Grace sowers
with wild abandon.

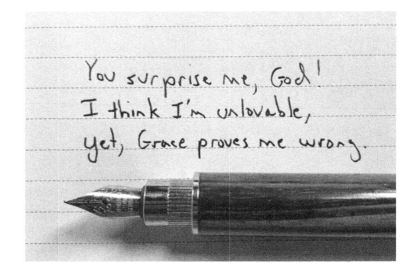

You surprise me, God!
I think I'm unlovable,
yet, Grace proves me wrong.

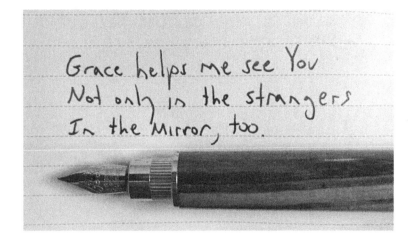

Grace helps me see You.
Not only in the strangers;
in the mirror, too.

I have privilege
which gives me a voice to use.
I use it for You.

I use it for You.
Help me lift up the oppressed
with words full of Grace

With words full of Grace
I will also listen, God
Help me hear others.

I have privilege
which gives me a voice to use.
I use it for You.

I use it for You.
Help me lift up the oppressed
with words full of Grace.

With words full of Grace
I will also listen, God.
Help me hear others.

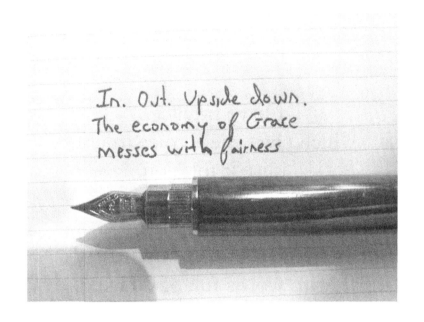

In. Out. Upside down.
The economy of Grace
messes with fairness.

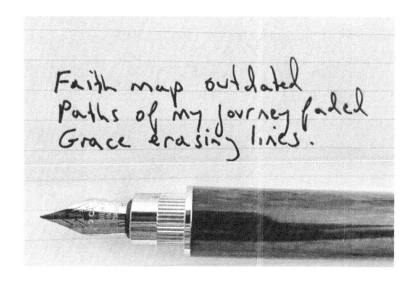

Faith map outdated.
Paths of my journey faded.
Grace erasing lines.

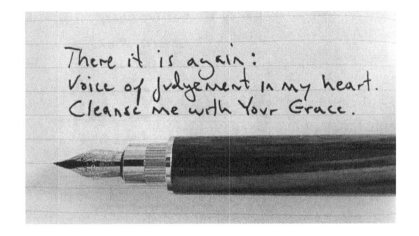

There it is again:
Voice of judgment in my heart.
Cleanse me with Your Grace.

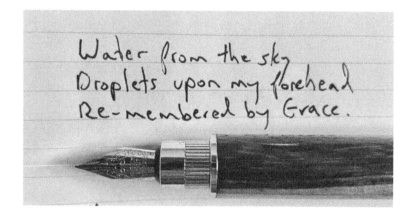

Water from the sky.
Droplets upon my forehead.
Re-membered by Grace.

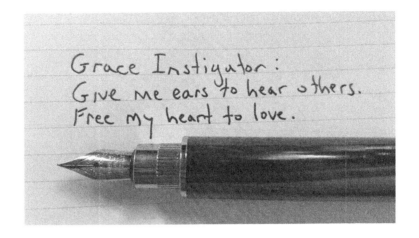

Grace Instigator:
Give me ears to hear others.
Free my heart to love.

Help me find the word
that capture my amazement.
Grace leaves me speechless.

Help me share the joy.
Help me find it when I can't.
Joy found in Your Grace.

Help me share the love
that I receive from You, God.
Love found in Your Grace.

Help me see the Hope
when eyes are blurry with tears.
Hope found in Your Grace.

I'm up for review.
My heart says I've failed again!
Thankful Grace goes last!

Guide my heart to love.
Help my feet walk in kindness.
Clothe me with Your Grace.

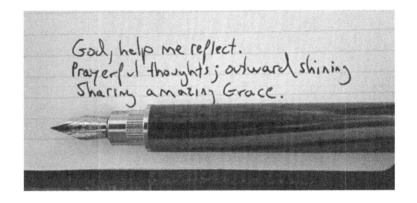

God, help me reflect.
Prayerful thoughts; outward shining.
Sharing amazing Grace.

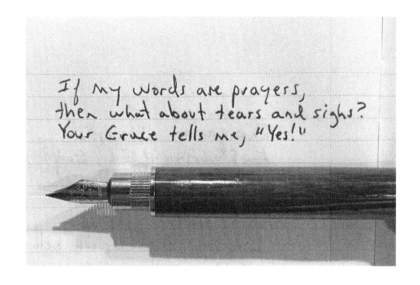

If my words are prayers,
then what about tears and sighs?
Your Grace tells me, "Yes!"

We are witnesses.
We have tasted Your Grace, God.
Help us share it, too.

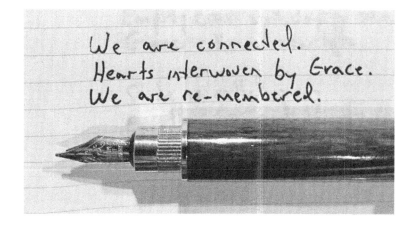

We are connected.
Hearts interwoven by Grace.
We are re-membered.

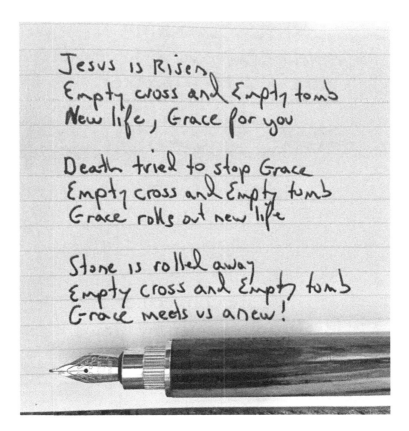

Jesus is Risen,
Empty cross and Empty tomb
New life, Grace for you

Death tried to stop Grace
Empty cross and Empty tomb
Grace rolls out new life

Stone is rolled away
Empty cross and Empty tomb
Grace meets us anew!

Jesus is risen.
Empty cross and Empty tomb.
New life, Grace for you.

Death tried to stop Grace.
Empty cross and empty tomb.
Grace rolls out new life.

Stone is rolled away.
Empty cross and empty tomb.
Grace meets us anew!

I accuse myself
I am not enough or loved,
Jesus says, "You're wrong!"

I accuse myself
My faith isn't strong enough.
Jesus laughs at this.

I accuse myself
Jesus says, "You are enough!"
"My Grace's sufficient"

I accuse myself.
I am not enough or loved.
Jesus says, "You're wrong!"

I accuse myself.
My faith isn't strong enough.
Jesus laughs at this.

I accuse myself.
Jesus says, "You are enough!"
"My Grace's sufficient."

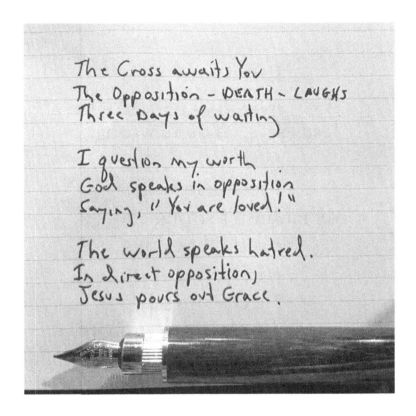

The Cross awaits You
The Opposition - DEATH - LAUGHS
Three Days of waiting

I question my worth
God speaks in opposition
Saying, " You are loved!"

The world speaks hatred.
In direct opposition,
Jesus pours out Grace.

The Cross awaits You.
The opposition – Death – LAUGHS.
Three days of waiting.

I question my worth.
God speaks in opposition,
saying, "You are loved!"

The world speaks hatred.
In direct opposition,
Jesus pours out Grace.

Here is the promise:
When I feel lost and alone,
God draws near to me.

God draws near to me
before I even know it.
The beauty of Grace!

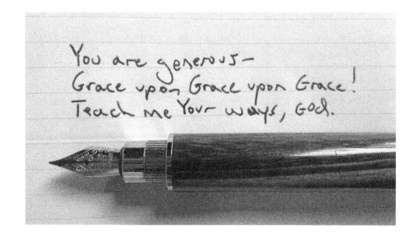

You are generous -
Grace upon Grace upon Grace!
Teach me Your ways, God.

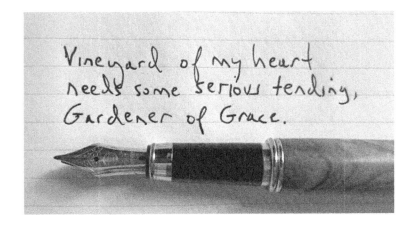

Vineyard of my heart
needs some serious tending,
Gardener of Grace.

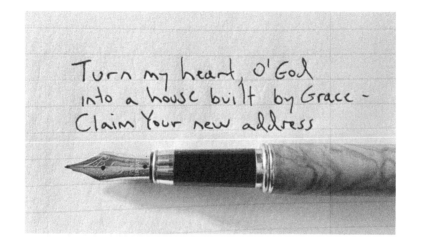

Turn my heart, O' God
into a house built by Grace -
Claim Your new address.

Help us to welcome
the kin-dom You are forming.
Grace shaped family.

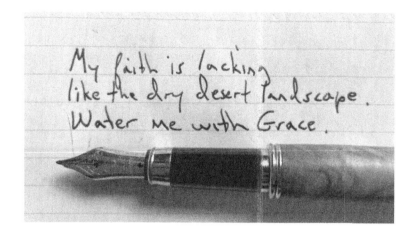

My faith is lacking
like the dry desert landscape.
Water me with Grace.

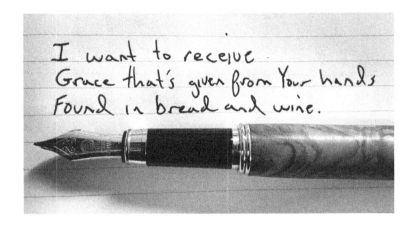

I want to receive
Grace that's given from Your hands
found in bread and wine.

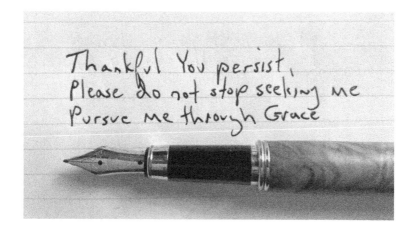

Thankful You persist.
Please do not stop seeking me.
Pursue me through Grace.

My heart has been crushed.
Life has been taken from me.
Your Grace restores me

Your Grace restores me.
When all hope becomes hopeless
You transform it all

You transform it all
The grave over-turned by Grace
I was made anew

Grace transforms my life
all I am; all I will be
Is because of Grace

My heart has been crushed.
Life has been taken from me.
Your Grace restores me.

Your Grace restores me.
When all hope becomes hopeless,
You transform it all.

You transform it all.
The grave overturned by Grace
I was made anew.

Grace transforms my life.
All I am; all I will be
is because of Grace.

Have mercy on me
Words echo within my heart
The Word pours out Grace

Your Mercy and Grace
are saving the entire world.
Help me remember.

Help me have mercy
on myself and my neighbor
Help me live out Grace

Have mercy on me.
Words echo within my heart.
The Word pours out Grace.

Your mercy and Grace
are saving the entire world.
Help me remember.

Help me have mercy
on myself and my neighbor.
Help me live out Grace.

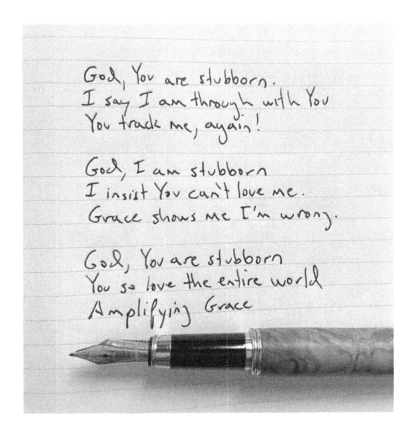

God, You are stubborn.
I say I am through with You
You track me, again!

God, I am stubborn
I insist You can't love me.
Grace shows me I'm wrong.

God, You are stubborn
You so love the entire world
Amplifying Grace

God, You are stubborn.
I say I am through with You.
You track me, again.

God, I am stubborn.
I insist You can't love me.
Grace shows me I'm wrong.

God, You are stubborn.
You so love the entire world.
Amplifying Grace.

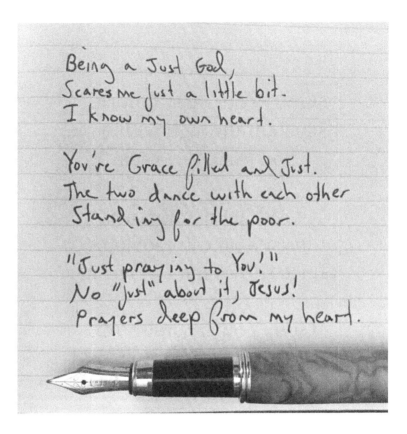

Being a Just God,
Scares me just a little bit.
I know my own heart.

You're Grace filled and Just.
The two dance with each other
Standing for the poor.

"Just praying to You!"
No "just" about it, Jesus!
Prayers deep from my heart.

Being a just God,
scares me just a little bit.
I know my own heart.

You're Grace filled and just.
The two dance with each other.
Standing for the poor.

"Just praying to You!"
No "just" about it, Jesus!
Prayers deep from my heart.

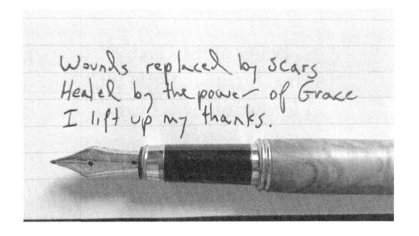

Wounds replaced by scars.
Healed by the power of Grace.
I lift up my thanks.

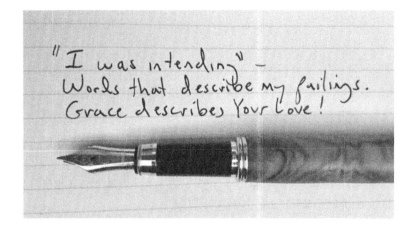

"I was intending" -
Words that describe my failings.
Grace describes Your love!

World is inviting
"Eye for an Eye is the way"
God, help me forgive.

Grace is inviting
Speaking to my shame filled heart
Offering me freedom

You're inviting me
To drop the shame I carry
and lean into Grace.

World is inviting.
"Eye for an Eye is the way."
God, help me forgive.

Grace is inviting.
Speaking to my shame filled heart.
Offering freedom.

You're inviting me
to drop the shame I carry
and lean into Grace.

Grace calls all lawful
Those who were out now are in.
You welcome us all.

You welcome us all
Please remind me: "All" means me.
Help me lean on You.

Help me lean on You.
God's Grace messes with my rules
God calls all lawful!

Grace calls all lawful.
Those who were out now are in.
You welcome us all.

You welcome us all.
Please remind me: "All" means me.
Help me lean on You.

Help me lean on You.
God's Grace messes with my rules.
God calls all lawful!

This question plagues me:
Am I worthy of love, God?
Grace reassures me!

God doesn't give up.
God says that we all belong.
We're worthy of Grace!

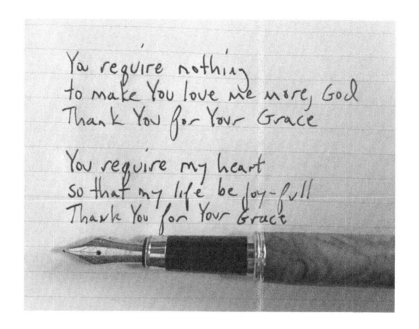

You require nothing
to make You love me more, God.
Thank You for Your Grace.

You require my heart
so that my life be joy-full.
Thank You for Your Grace.

I need Your help God
My heart is full of worry
Please replace with Grace

So much worry, God
It finds ways through my armor
Please replace with Grace

Worry's a virus
It takes over all my thoughts
Please replace with Grace

I need Your help, God.
My heart is full of worry.
Please replace with Grace.

So much worry, God.
It finds ways through my armor.
Please replace with Grace.

Worry's a virus.
It takes over all my thoughts.
Please replace with Grace.

All my possessions
mean nothing compared to this:
The Gift of God's Grace

My God, please help me.
I'm possessed by possessions
Help free me from them.

God says I'm enough
Not through all my possessions
But rather, God's Grace!

All my possessions
mean nothing compared to this:
The Gift of God's Grace.

My God, please help me.
I'm possessed by possessions.
Help free me from them.

God says I'm enough.
Not through all my possessions.
But rather, God's Grace!

Woe is me, I say
Woe to all those who cross me
And yet, You love me.

My well founded woe
Can be important lament
For that - Thank You, God

Grace turns me around
Changes my woe into WOAH!
Grace shows You love me.

Woe is me, I say.
Woe to all those who cross me.
And yet, You love me.

My well founded woe
can be important lament.
For that – Thank You God.

Grace turns me around.
Changes my woe to WOAH!
Grace shows You love me.

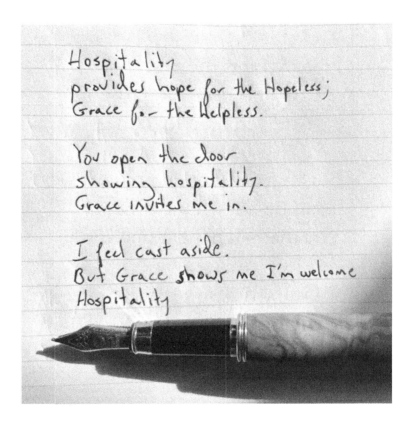

Hospitality
provides hope for the Hopeless;
Grace for the Helpless.

You open the door
showing hospitality.
Grace invites me in.

I feel cast aside.
But Grace shows me I'm welcome
Hospitality

Hospitality
provides hope for the Hopeless;
Grace for the Helpless.

You open the door
showing hospitality.
Grace invites me in.

I feel cast aside,
but Grace shows me I'm welcome.
Hospitality.

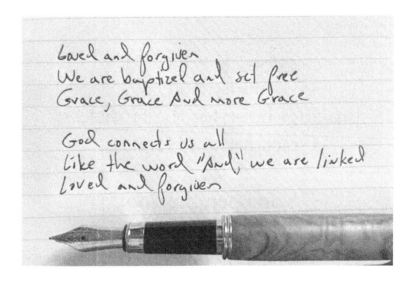

Love and forgiven.
We are baptized and set free.
Grace, Grace and more Grace.

God connects us all.
Like the word "And," we are linked.
Loved and forgiven.

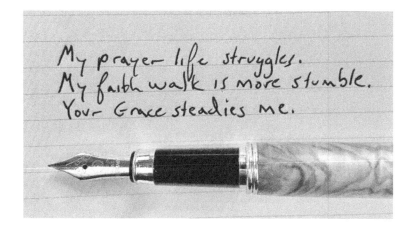

My prayer life struggles.
My faith walk is more stumble.
Your Grace steadies me.

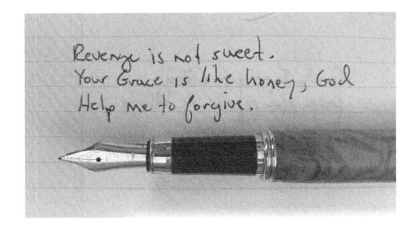

Revenge is not sweet.
Your Grace is like honey, God.
Help me to forgive.

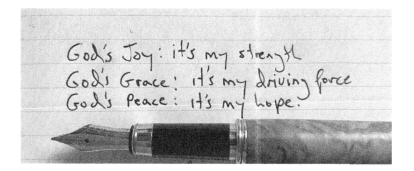

God's Joy: It's my strength.
God's Grace: It's my driving force.
God's Peace: It's my hope.

Transform my heart, God.
Pull back the veil that hides You.
Grace, illuminate!

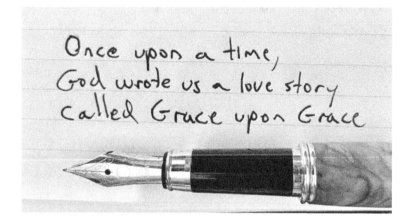

Once upon a time,
God wrote us a love story,
called Grace upon Grace.

I'm struggling, God
Mood swings - from smiling to tears
Wrap me in Your Grace.

I'm struggling, God
Faith wavers, as do my prayers
Wrap me in Your Grace.

I'm struggling, God
Remind me that I'm enough
Wrap me in Your Grace.

I'm struggling God.
Mood swings – from smiling to tears.
Wrap me in Your Grace.

I'm struggling, God.
Faith wavers, as do my prayers.
Wrap me in Your Grace.

I'm struggling, God.
Remind me that I'm enough.
Wrap me in Your Grace.

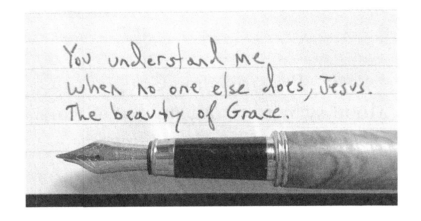

You understand me
when no one else does, Jesus.
The beauty of Grace.

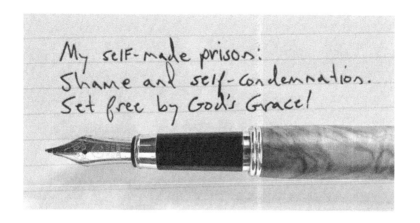

My self-made prison:
Shame and self-condemnation.
Set free by God's Grace!

Grace is offensive
You love with wild abandon
It is confusing

It is confusing
Yet, I am quite thankful, God
Your Grace includes me.

Your Grace includes me!
Grace includes my enemies.
Grace is offensive!

Grace is offensive.
You love with wild abandon.
It is confusing.

It is confusing.
Yet, I am quite thankful, God
Your Grace includes me!

Your Grace includes me!
Grace includes my enemies.
Grace is offensive!

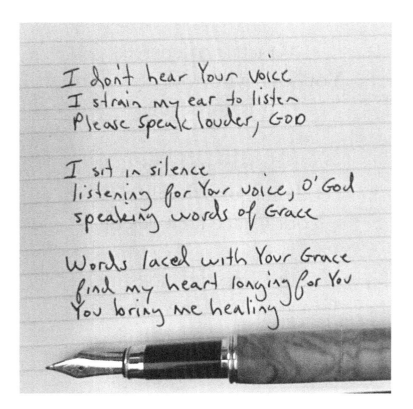

I don't hear Your voice
I strain my ear to listen
Please speak louder, GOD

I sit in silence
listening for Your voice, O'God
speaking words of Grace

Words laced with Your Grace
find my heart longing for You
You bring me healing

I don't hear Your voice.
I strain my ear to listen.
Please speak louder, God.

I sit in silence
listening for Your voice, O' God,
speaking words of Grace.

Word laced with Your Grace
find my heart heart longing for You.
You bring me healing.

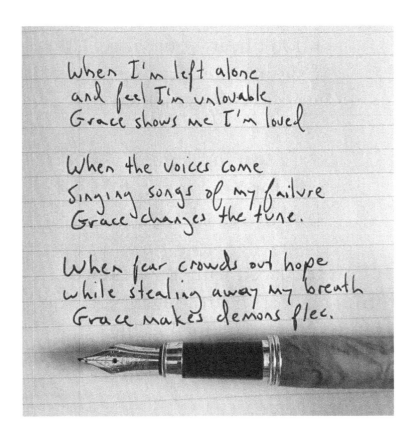

When I'm left alone
and feel I'm unlovable
Grace shows me I'm loved

When the voices come
Singing songs of my failure
Grace changes the tune.

When fear crowds out hope
while stealing away my breath
Grace makes demons flee.

When I'm left alone
and feel I'm unlovable.
Grace shows me I'm loved.

When the voices come,
singing songs of my failure.
Grace changes the tune.

When fear crowds out hope
while stealing away my breath.
Grace makes demons flee.

The playlist called, "Grace"
is on eternal repeat!
It's on God's "Best of".

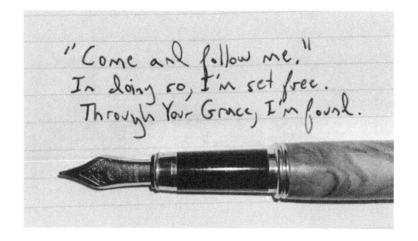

"Come and follow me."
In doing so, I'm set free.
Through Your Grace, I'm found.

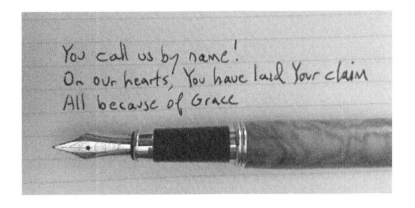

You call us by name!
On our hearts, You've laid Your claim.
All because of Grace.

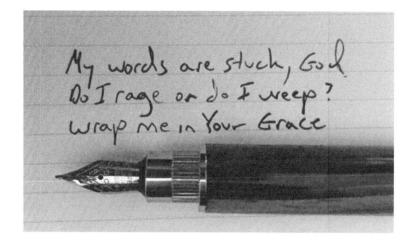

My words are stuck, God.
Do I rage or do I weep?
Wrap me in Your Grace.

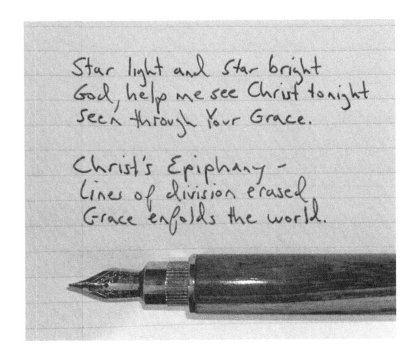

Star light and Star bright
God, help me see Christ tonight
looking through Your Grace.

Christ's Epiphany -
Lines of division erased.
Grace enfolds the world.

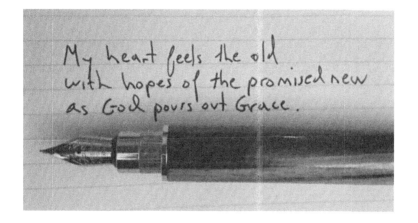

My heart feels the old
with hopes of the promised new
as God pours out Grace.

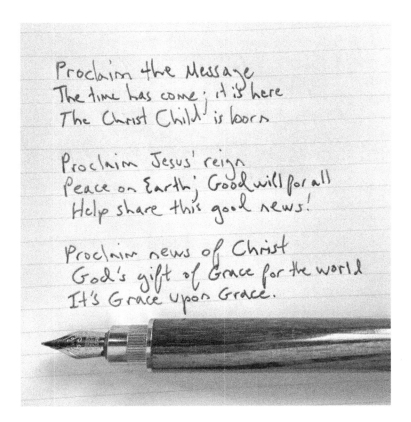

Proclaim the Message
The time has come; it is here
The Christ Child is born

Proclaim Jesus' reign
Peace on Earth; Goodwill for all
Help share this good news!

Proclaim news of Christ
God's gift of Grace for the world
It's Grace upon Grace.

Proclaim the Message.
The time has come; it is here.
The Christ Child is born.

Proclaim Jesus' reign.
Peace on Earth; Good will for all.
Help share this good news!

Proclaim news of Christ.
God's gift of Grace for the world.
It's Grace upon Grace.

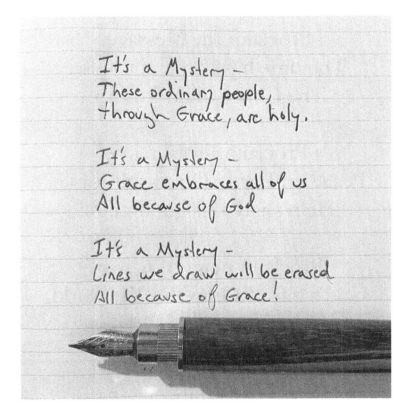

It's a Mystery –
These ordinary people,
through Grace, are holy.

It's a Mystery –
Grace embraces all of us
All because of God

It's a Mystery –
Lines we draw will be erased
All because of Grace!

It's a Mystery -
These ordinary people,
through Grace, are holy.

It's a Mystery -
Grace embraces all of us.
All because of God.

It's a Mystery -
Lines we draw will be erased.
All because of Grace!

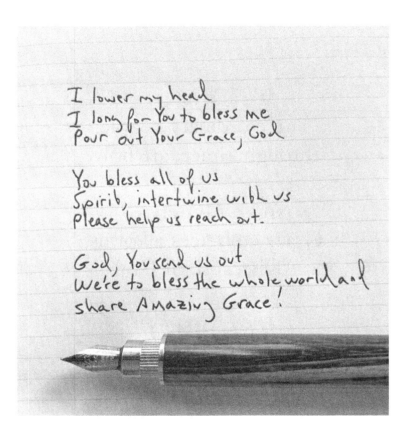

I lower my head
I long for You to bless me
Pour out Your Grace, God

You bless all of us
Spirit, intertwine with us
Please help us reach out.

God, You send us out
We're to bless the whole world and
share Amazing Grace!

I lower my head.
I long for You to bless me.
Pour out Your Grace, God.

You bless all of us.
Spirit, intertwine with us.
Please help us reach out.

God, You send us out.
We're to bless the whole world and
share Amazing Grace!

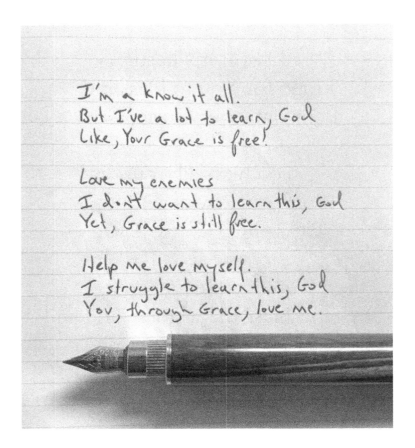

I'm a know it all.
But I've a lot to learn, God
Like, Your Grace is free!

Love my enemies
I don't want to learn this, God
Yet, Grace is still free.

Help me love myself.
I struggle to learn this, God
You, through Grace, love me.

I'm a know it all.
But I've a lot to learn, God.
Like, Your Grace is free.

Love my enemies.
I don't want to learn this, God.
Yet, Grace is still free.

Help me love myself.
I struggle to learn this, God.
You, through Grace, love me.

Heavy steps feel light.
My hardened heart softens, too.
God's Grace renews me!

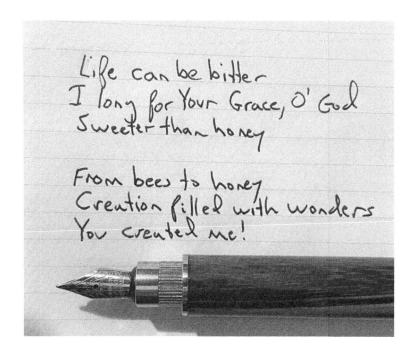

Life can be bitter.
I long for Your Grace, O' God.
Sweeter than honey.

From bees to honey.
Creation filled with wonders.
You created me!

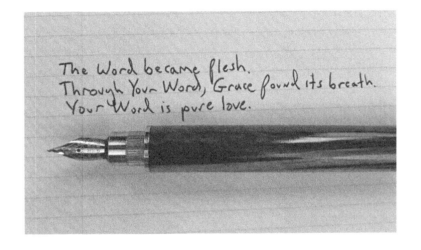

The Word became flesh.
Through Your Word, Grace found its breath.
Your Word is pure love.

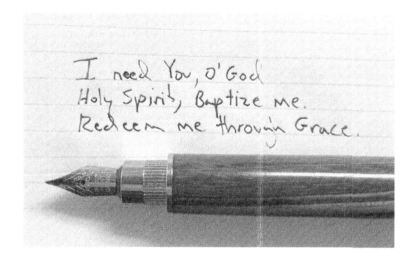

I need You, O' God.
Holy Spirit, baptize me.
Redeem me through Grace.

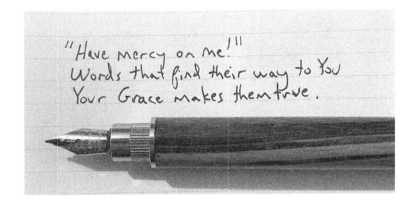

"Have mercy on me!"
Words that find their way to You.
Your Grace makes them true.

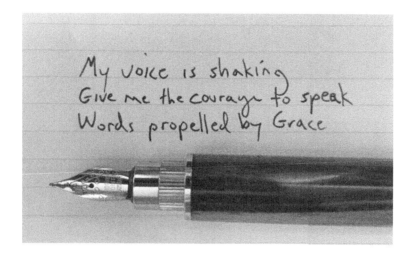

My voice is shaking.
Give me the courage to speak.
Words propelled by Grace.

Fellowship of God
People gathered by Your Grace
to better the world!

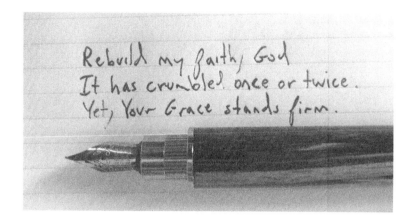

Rebuild my faith, God.
It has crumbled once or twice.
Yet, Your Grace stands firm.

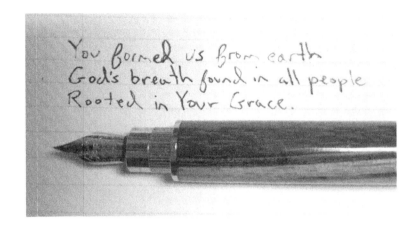

You formed us from earth.
God's breath found in all people.
Rooted in Your Grace.

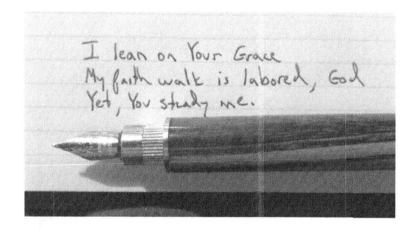

I lean on Your Grace.
My faith walk is labored, God.
Yet, You steady me.

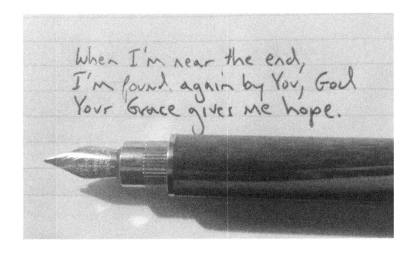

When I'm near the end,
I'm found again by You, God.
Your Grace gives me hope.

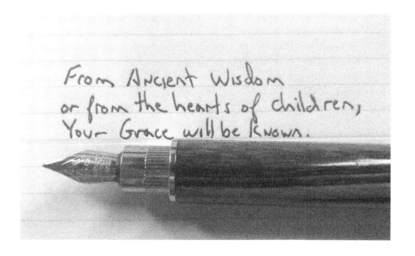

From Ancient Wisdom
or from the hearts of children,
Your Grace will be known.

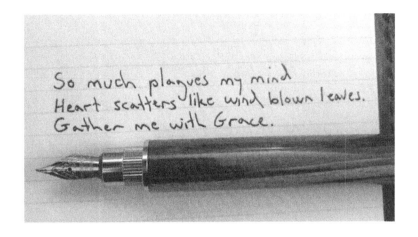

So much plagues my mind.
Heart scatters like wind blown leaves.
Gather me with Grace.

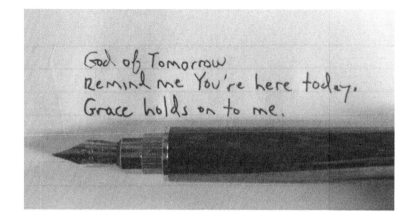

God of Tomorrow.
Remind me You're here today.
Grace holds on to me.

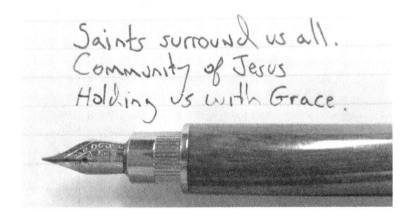

Saints surround us all.
Community of Jesus
holding us with Grace.

Grace is not a trick.
Undeserved love is a treat!
Help me share Your love.

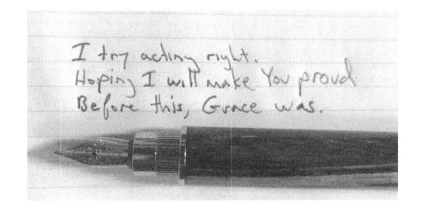

I try acting right.
Hoping I will make You proud.
Before this, Grace was.

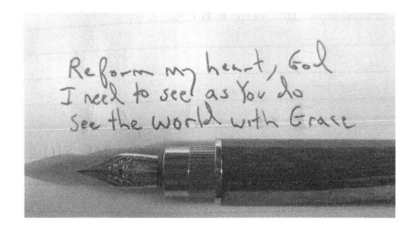

Reform my heart, God.
I need to see as You do.
See the world with Grace.

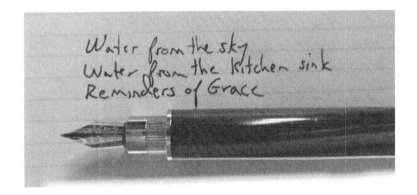

Water from the sky.
Water from the kitchen sink.
Reminders of Grace.

When I feel most lost,
with hope blown around like dust,
Grace comes and finds me.

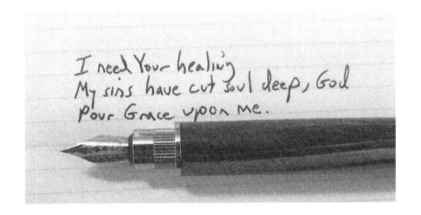

I need Your healing.
My sins have cut soul deep, God.
Pour Grace upon me.

Blooper reel plays loud
reminding me of failures.
Grace speaks love louder!

Take Grace for granted!
The love of God is secure.
Christ never quits you.

Grace flows out freely.
This table Jesus has set
has a place for you!

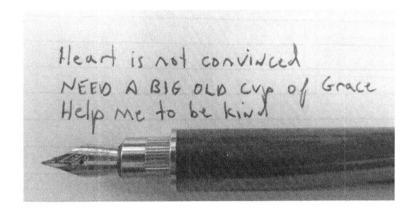

Heart is not convinced.
Need a BIG OLD CUP of Grace.
Help me to be kind.

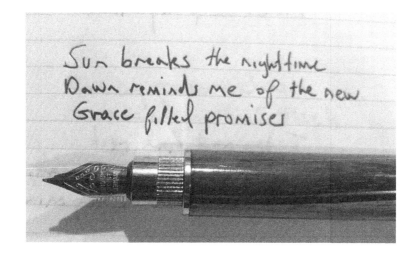

Sun breaks the night time.
Dawn reminds me of the new.
Grace filled promises.

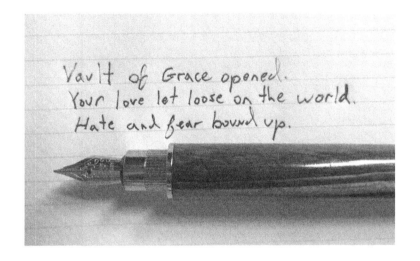

Vault of Grace opened.
Your love let loose on the world.
Hate and fear bound up.

I await answers.
Questions and doubts seek me out.
Yet, so does Your Grace.

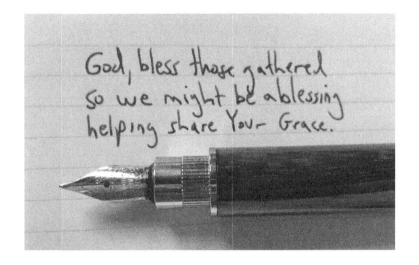

God, bless those gathered
so we might be a blessing
help share Your Grace.

Nothing separates.
Heart feels alienated.
Grace re-members me.

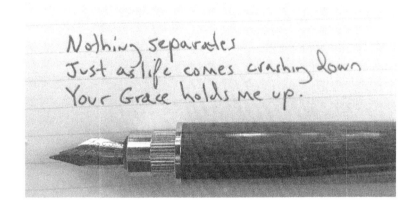

Nothing separates.
Just as life comes crashing down,
Your Grace holds me up.

Nothing separates.
Even when I think I'm through,
Grace says, "I love you!"

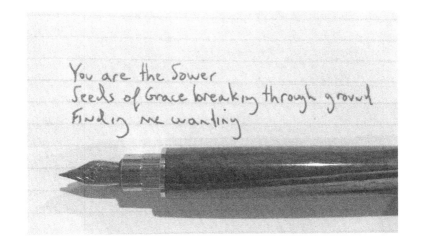

You are the Sower.
Seeds of Grace breaking through ground,
finding me wanting.

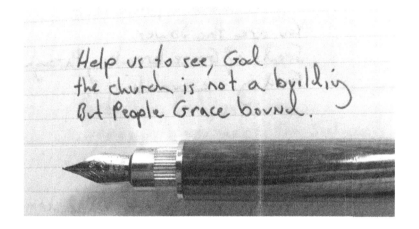

Help us to see, God,
the church is not a building,
but people Grace bound.

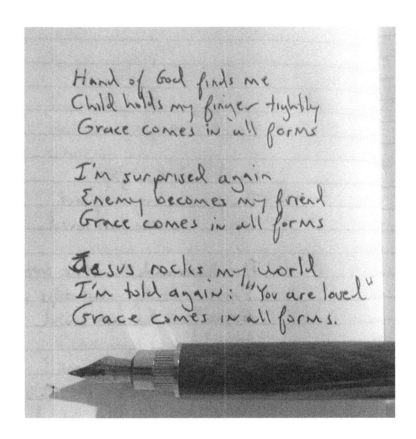

Hand of God finds me
Child holds my finger tightly
Grace comes in all forms

I'm surprised again
Enemy becomes my friend
Grace comes in all forms

Jesus rocks my world
I'm told again: "You are loved"
Grace comes in all forms.

Hand of God finds me.
Child holds my finger tightly.
Grace comes in all forms.

I'm surprised again.
Enemy becomes my friend.
Grace comes in all forms.

Jesus rocks my world.
I'm told again: "You are loved."
Grace comes in all forms.

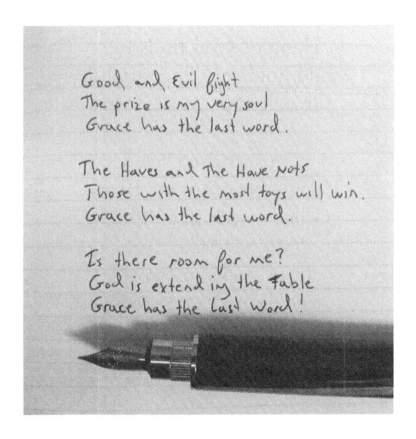

Good and Evil fight
The prize is my very soul
Grace has the last word.

The Haves and The Have Nots
Those with the most toys will win.
Grace has the last word.

Is there room for me?
God is extending the Fable
Grace has the last Word!

Good and evil fight.
The prize is my very soul.
Grace has the last word.

The Haves and the Have Nots
Those with the most toys will win.
Grace has the last word.

Is there room for me?
God's extending the table.
Grace has the last word!

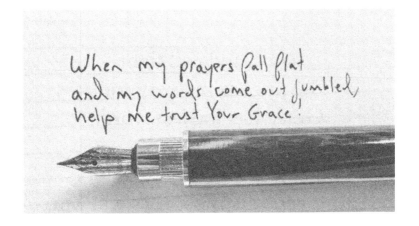

When my prayers fall flat
and my words come out jumbled,
help me trust Your Grace!

Don't have much to give.
My coffers seem depleted.
Fill me with Your Grace.

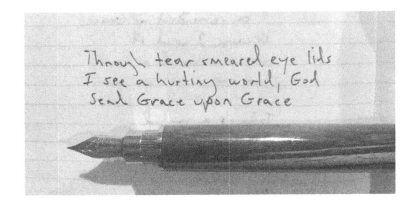

Through tear smeared eye lids,
I see a hurting world, God.
Send Grace upon Grace.

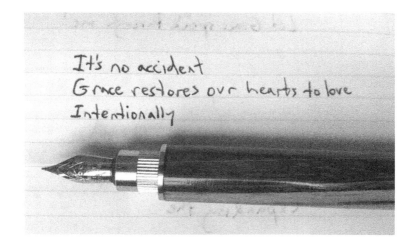

It's no accident.
Grace restores our hearts to love -
intentionally.

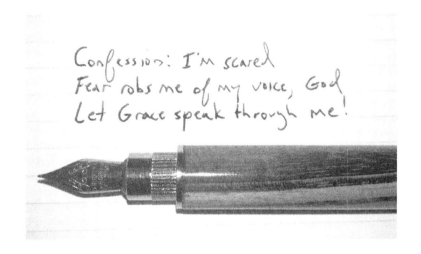

Confession: I'm scared.
Fear robs me of my voice, God.
Let Grace speak through me!

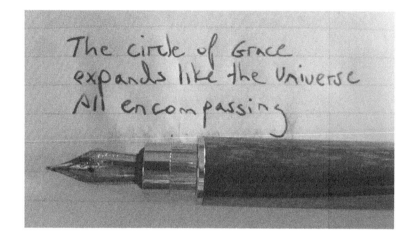

The circle of Grace
expands like the Universe.
All encompassing.

You have sent us out
as conspirators of Grace
loving Your people!

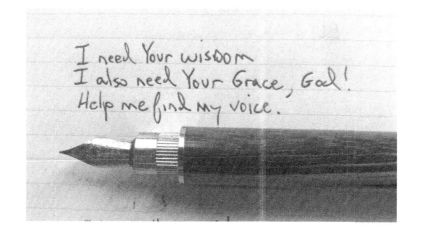

I need Your wisdom.
I also need Your Grace, God!
Help me find my voice.

O' Woman Wisdom,
Speak to my heart words of Grace.
Calm my troubled soul.

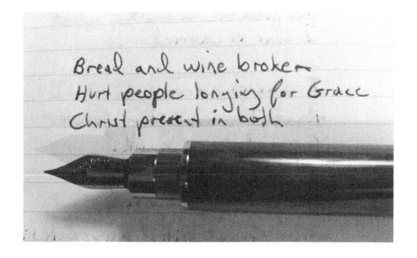

Bread and wine broken.
Hurt people longing for Grace.
Christ present in both.

Give me ears to hear
Help me listen to the cries.
Your heart full of Grace

Your heart full of Grace
I know You listen, o' God
with deep compassion

with deep compassion
Help me listen for Your Grace
Give me ~~ears~~ to hear
           ears

Give me ears to hear.
Help me listen to the cries.
Your heart full of Grace.

Your heart full of Grace.
I know You listen, O' God,
With deep compassion.

With deep compassion,
help me listen for Your Grace.
Give me ears to hear.

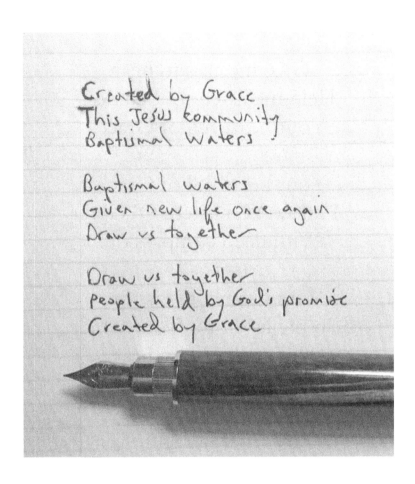

Created by Grace
This Jesus community
Baptismal waters!

Baptismal waters
Given new life once again
Draw us together

Draw us together
People held by God's promise
Created by Grace

Created by Grace.
This Jesus community.
Baptismal waters.

Baptismal waters.
Given new life once again.
Draw us together.

Draw us together.
People held by God's promise.
Created by Grace.

We are bathed by Grace
I am seeing changes, God
as my heart softens.

As my heart softens,
I hope I'm seeing others
As You love us all.

As You love us all;
Seeing we need Your healing,
We are bathed by Grace.

We are bathed by Grace.
I am seeing changes, God,
as my heart softens.

As my heart softens,
I hope I'm seeing others,
as You love us all.

As You love us all;
seeing we need Your healing,
we are bathed by Grace.

Our testimony:
Living out the love of God
Reaching out to all

Reaching out to all
with Grace filled testimony
Preaching through action

Preaching through action
Deeds expressing Your love, God
Our testimony!

Our testimony:
Living out the love of God.
Reaching out to all.

Reaching out to all
with Grace filled testimony.
Preaching through action.

Preaching through action.
Deeds expressing Your love, God.
Our testimony!

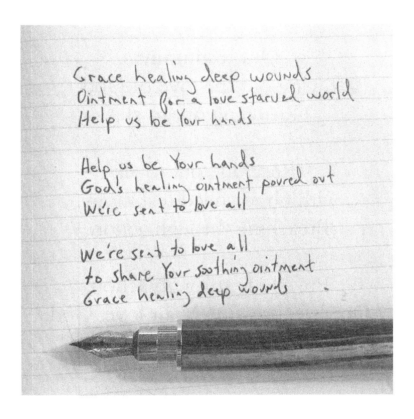

Grace healing deep wounds
Ointment for a love starved world
Help us be Your hands

Help us be Your hands
God's healing ointment poured out
We're sent to love all

We're sent to love all
to share Your soothing ointment
Grace healing deep wounds

Grace healing deep wounds.
Ointment for a love starved world.
Help us be Your hands.

Help us be Your hands.
God's healing ointment poured out.
We're sent to love all.

We're sent to love all
to share Your soothing ointment.
Grace healing deep wounds.

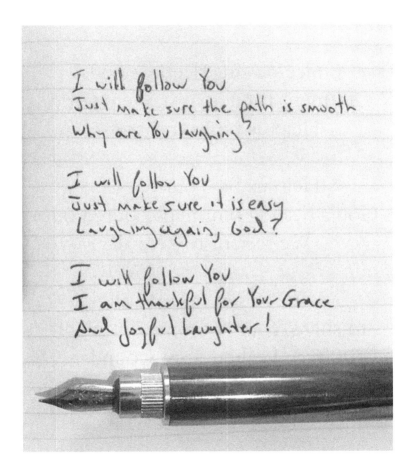

I will follow You
Just make sure the path is smooth
Why are You laughing?

I will follow You
Just make sure it is easy
Laughing again, God?

I will follow You
I am thankful for Your Grace
And joyful laughter!

I will follow You.
Just make sure the path is smooth.
Why are You laughing?

I will follow You.
Just make sure it is easy.
Laughing again, God?

I will follow You.
I am thankful for Your Grace,
and joyful laughter!

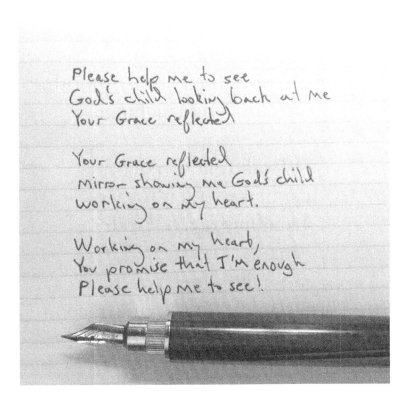

Please help me to see
God's child looking back at me
Your Grace reflected

Your Grace reflected
Mirror showing me God's child
working on my heart.

Working on my heart,
You promise that I'm enough
Please help me to see!

Please help me to see.
God's child looking back at me.
Your Grace reflected.

Your Grace reflected.
Mirror showing me God's child,
working on my heart.

Working on my heart,
You promise that I'm enough.
Please help me to see!

My eyes don't see You
Yet, You stroll with me, Jesus
Questions while we walk

Questions while we walk
helping me ponder Your way
Breaking of the Bread

Breaking of the Bread
I see Grace poured out for us.
Recognizing You!

My eyes don't see You.
Yet, You stroll with me, Jesus.
Questions while we walk.

Questions while we walk,
helping me ponder Your way.
Breaking of the bread.

Breaking of the bread.
I see Grace poured out for us.
Recognizing You!

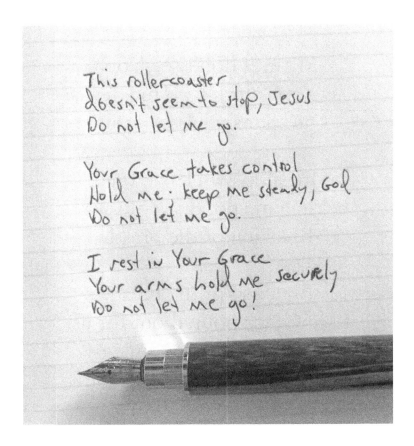

This rollercoaster
doesn't seem to stop, Jesus
Do not let me go.

Your Grace takes control
Hold me; keep me steady, God
Do not let me go.

I rest in Your Grace
Your arms hold me securely
Do not let me go!

This roller coaster
doesn't seem to stop, Jesus.
Do not let me go.

Your Grace takes control.
Hold me; keep me steady, God.
Do not let me go.

I rest in Your Grace.
Your arms hold me securely.
Do not let me go!

The Wooden Cross looms
You're present with two or three
A flash mob of Grace

A flash mob of Grace
made up of Your Children, God
Living out Your love

Living out Your love
as You stand before a mob
The Wooden Cross looms

The wooden cross looms.
You're present with two or three.
A flash mob of Grace.

A flash mob of Grace
made up of Your children, God.
Living out Your love.

Living out Your love
as You stand before a mob.
The wooden cross looms.

As fear rises up
Help me hold fast to Grace, God
Assurance of love

Assurance of love
Help me fast from shame stories
Remind me through Grace

Remind me through Grace:
Hold fast to God's promises,
as fear rises up!

As fear rises up,
help me hold fast to Grace, God.
Assurance of love.

Assurance of love.
Help me fast from shame stories.
Remind me through Grace.

Remind me through Grace:
Hold fast to God's promises,
as fear rises up!

God, wrap me in love
Chosen to be a blessing
Help me live through You

Help me live through You
You have chosen the whole world
on whom to pour Grace

On whom to pour Grace?
I hope that I am chosen.
God, wrap me in love.

God, wrap me in love.
Chosen to be a blessing.
Help me live through You.

Help me live through You.
You have chosen the whole world
on whom to pour Grace.

On whom to pour Grace?
I hope that I am chosen.
God, wrap me in love.

Every breath I take
I am reminded of GRACE
God, You changed my life.

Grace rewrites the scene
Grace repairs the splitting seam
Grace heals my hurt heart

We are Grace infused.
Though, sometimes we are confused,
You still pour out Grace!

Every breath I take,
I am reminded of Grace.
God, You changed my life.

Grace rewrites the scene.
Grace repairs the splitting seam.
Grace heals my hurt heart.

We are Grace infused.
Though, sometimes we are confused.
You still pour out Grace!

Purify my heart.
Melt away the frozen hurts
Embedded within.

Embedded within
sacred cows; these hollow words
melt and fade away

"Melt and fade away."
Grace speaks to the Winter Queen
Purify my heart.

Purify my heart.
Melt away the frozen hurts.
Embedded within.

Embedded within.
Sacred cows; these hollow words
melt and fade away.

"Melt and fade away!"
Grace speaks to the Winter Queen.
Purify my heart.

There seems a bounty
On my heart, my soul, my life!
World seems to attack!

World seems to attack!
Yet, Your bounty of Grace, God
loves abundantly

Love, abundantly,
pours upon Your creation;
Yes, there's a bounty!

There seems a bounty
on my heart, my soul, my life!
World seems to attack!

World seems to attack!
Yet, Your bounty of Grace, God
loves abundantly.

Love, abundantly,
pours upon Your creation;
Yes, there's a bounty!

It is four a.m.
My brain reminds me I failed
God, help me forget

God, help me forget
All the shame that plagues my dreams
Feel me with Your Grace

Feel me with Your Grace
Help me not forget this when
It is four a.m.

It is four a.m.
My brain reminds me I failed.
God, help me forget.

God, help me forget
all the shame that plagues my dreams.
Feed me with Your Grace.

Feed me with Your Grace.
Help me not forget this when
it is four a.m.

Reflection of Grace
seen on God's children's faces
gives me renewed hope.

Reflection of Grace
Mirror Mirror on the wall
God's love is for all

Reflection of Grace
Lights up my path like a lamp
God's word in the flesh!

Reflection of Grace
seen on God's children's faces
gives me renewed hope.

Reflection of Grace.
Mirror Mirror on the Wall
God's love is for all.

Reflection of Grace
lights up my path like a lamp.
God's word in the flesh!

I like to wander.
God, please keep me close to You,
tethered by Your Grace.

Tethered by Your Grace,
help me keep others in mind.
Common humanity

Common humanity
You keep reaching out with Grace
Pulling the world close.

I like to wander.
God, please keep me close to You,
tethered by Your Grace.

Tethered by Your Grace,
help me keep others in mind.
Common humanity.

Common humanity.
You keep reaching out with Grace.
Pulling the world close.

Your love never fails.
Your love embraces through Grace.
Thank You for Your love.

Thank You for Your love.
Your Grace pulls us together.
Love shows all, we're Yours!

Love shows all we're Yours!
Grace makes Your promises true.
Your love never fails!

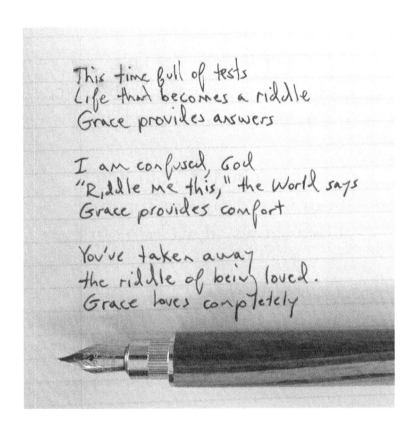

This time full of tests
Life that becomes a riddle
Grace provides answers

I am confused, God
"Riddle me this," the World says
Grace provides comfort

You've taken away
the riddle of being loved.
Grace loves completely

This time full of tests.
Life that becomes a riddle.
Grace provides answers.

I am confused, God.
"Riddle me this," the world says.
Grace provides comfort.

You've taken away
the riddle of being loved.
Grace loves completely.

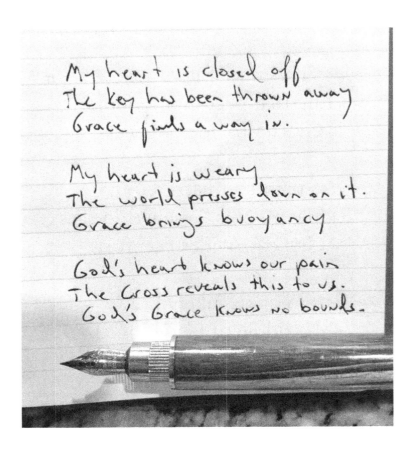

My heart is closed off.
The key has been thrown away.
Grace finds a way in.

My heart is weary.
The world presses down on it.
Grace brings buoyancy.

God's heart knows our pain.
The cross reveals this to us.
God's Grace knows no bounds.

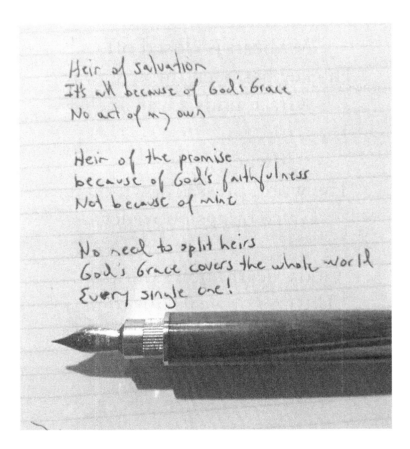

Heir of salvation
It's all because of God's Grace
No act of my own

Heir of the promise
because of God's faithfulness
Not because of mine

No need to split heirs
God's Grace covers the whole world
Every single one!

Heir of salvation.
It's all because of God's Grace.
No act of my own.

Heir of the promise
because of God's faithfulness
not because of mine.

No need to split heirs.
God's Grace covers the whole world.
Every single one!

I long to recieve
the promise that I'm enough
Help me believe that!

I long to recieve
Grace found around the table
Grace found in Your love

I long to recieve
Grace found within the neighbors
Your community

244

I long to receive
the promise that I'm enough.
Help me believe that!

I long to receive
Grace found around the table.
Grace found in Your love.

I long to receive
Grace found within the neighbor.
Your community.

Descend like a dove
The Heavens opening wide
Your voice of Grace speaks

Your voice of Grace speaks
"You are my be-lov-ed child!"
Grace infused waters

Grace infused waters
help recall promises that
Descend like a Dove.

Descend like a dove.
The Heavens opening wide.
Your voice of Grace speaks.

Your voice of Grace speaks,
"You are my be-lov-ed child!"
Grace infused waters.

Grace infused waters
help recall promises that
descend like a dove.

Like the sunrises
I have witnessed in my life:
You are awesome, God!

A baby's laughter
will remind me of this truth:
You are awesome, God!

Grace claims me again,
holding me close, whispering,
"You are awesome, kid!"

Like the sunrises
I have witnessed in my life:
You are awesome, God!

A baby's laughter
will remind me of this truth:
You are awesome, God!

Grace claims me again,
holding me close, whispering,
"You are awesome, Kid!"

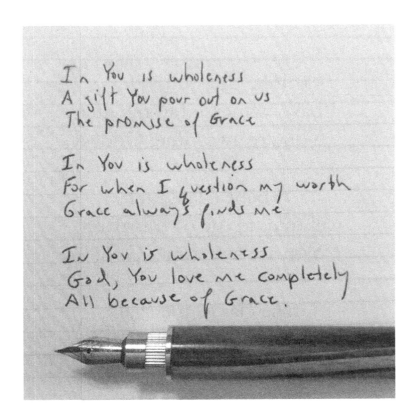

In You is wholeness
A gift You pour out on us
The promise of Grace

In You is wholeness
For when I question my worth
Grace always finds me

In You is wholeness
God, You love me completely
All because of Grace.

In You is wholeness.
A gift You pour out on us.
The promise of Grace.

In You is wholeness.
For when I question my worth,
Grace always finds me.

In You is wholeness.
God, You love me completely.
All because of Grace.

One word will bring life
One word cuts me to the quick
Your Word creates Grace

My word has power
to build up or to tear down.
Your Word creates Grace.

Our words need guidance
Help us hear Your word spoken.
You're the living Word.

One Word will bring life.
One word cuts me to the quick.
Your Word creates Grace.

My word has power
to build up or to tear down.
Your Word creates Grace.

Our words need guidance.
Help us hear Your word spoken.
You're the Living Word.

My tongue can be sharp
My tongue can heal others, too
Give me Grace filled words

I can speak of You
Love can be an unknown tongue
Give me Grace filled words

God, my tongue is parched
Living water helps me speak
Give me Grace filled words.

My tongue can be sharp.
My tongue can heal others, too.
Give me Grace filled words.

I can speak of You.
Love can be an unknown tongue.
Give me Grace filled words.

God, my tongue is parched.
Living water helps me speak.
Give me Grace filled words.

I am wide awake
to the failings of my heart
Wake me to Your Grace

I am wide awake
seeing my need for Your Grace.
Help me see You, God

I am wide awake
feeling Your warmth of Grace, God
By Your Grace, I'm woke!

I am wide awake
to the failing of my heart.
Wake me to Your Grace.

I am wide awake
seeing my need for Your Grace.
Help me see You, God.

I am wide awake
feeling Your warmth of Grace, God.
By Your Grace, I'm woke!

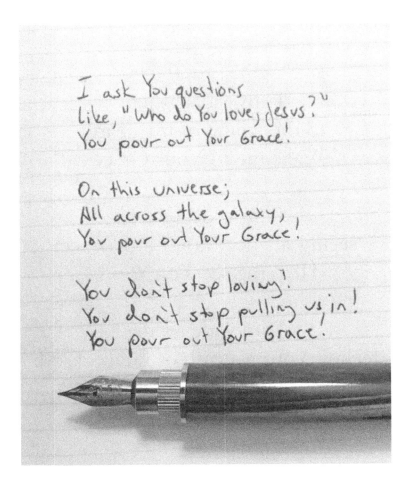

I ask You questions
Like, "Who do You love, Jesus?"
You pour out Your Grace!

On this universe;
All across the galaxy,
You pour out Your Grace!

You don't stop loving!
You don't stop pulling us in!
You pour out Your Grace.

I ask You questions
Like, "Who do You love, Jesus?"
You pour out Your Grace.

On this universe;
All across the galaxy,
You pour out Your Grace!

You don't stop loving!
You don't stop pulling us in!
You pour out Your Grace!

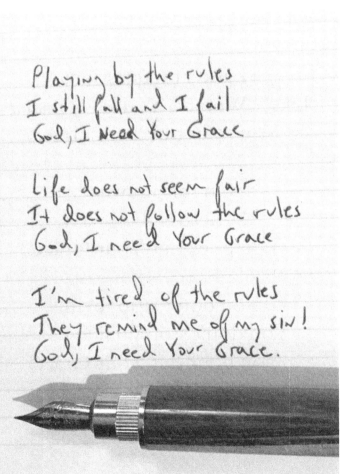

Playing by the rules
I still fall and I fail
God, I need Your Grace

Life does not seem fair
It does not follow the rules
God, I need Your Grace

I'm tired of the rules
They remind me of my sin!
God, I need Your Grace.

Playing by the rules,
I still fall and I fail.
God, I need Your Grace.

Life does not seem fair.
It does not follow the rules.
God, I need Your Grace.

I'm tired of the rules.
The remind me of my sin!
God, I need Your Grace.

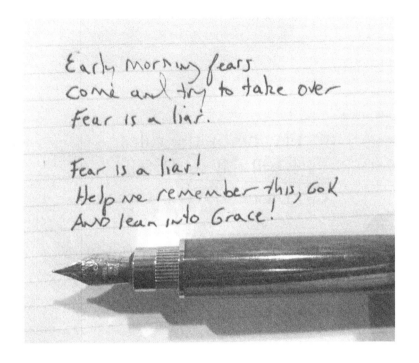

Early morning fears
come and try to take over.
Fear is a liar.

Fear is a liar!
Help me remember this, God.
And lean into Grace!

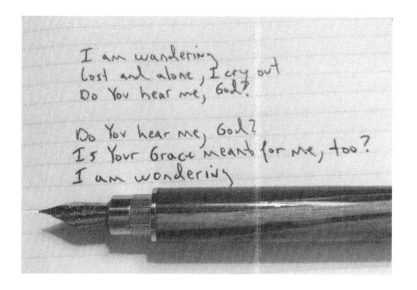

I am wandering.
Lost and alone, I cry out.
Do You hear me, God?

Do You hear me, God?
Is Your Grace mean for me, too?
I am wondering.

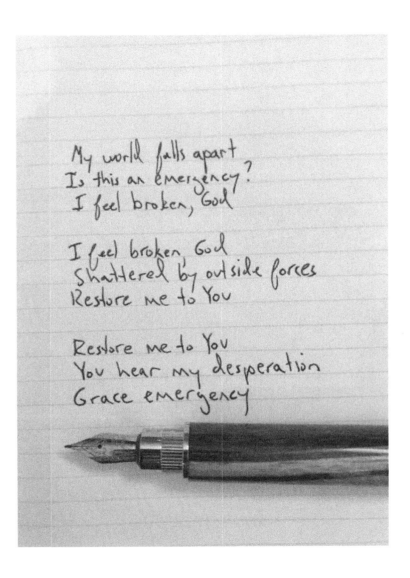

My world falls apart,
Is this an emergency?
I feel broken, God

I feel broken, God
Shattered by outside forces
Restore me to You

Restore me to You
You hear my desperation
Grace emergency

My world falls apart.
Is this an emergency?
I feel broken, God.

I feel broken, God.
Shattered by outside forces.
Restore me to You.

Restore me to You.
You hear my desperation.
Grace emergency.

Drums of Heaven call
Rush of the wind beckons us
We're given new life

We're given new life
Surrounded by Your music
Hearts echo Your song

Hearts echo Your song
When two or more are gathered
Grace asks for this dance

Drums of Heaven call.
Rush of the wind beckons us.
We're given new life.

We're given new life.
Surrounded by Your music.
Hearts echo Your song.

Hearts echo Your song.
When two or more are gathered.
Grace asks for this dance.

Today's a good day
to be reminded of Grace.
I've fallen again.

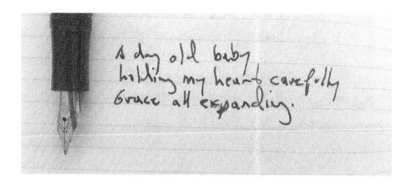

A day old baby
holding my heart carefully.
Grace all expanding.

Be-lov-ed, You're loved
May the Grace of God hold you
Be light for the world.

Be light for the world
Christ, God's Be-lov-ed, has come
Found in the manger.

Found in the manger,
Grace born for humanity
Be-lov-ed, You're loved!

Be-lov-ed, You're loved.
May the Grace of God hold you.
Be light for the world.

Be light for the world.
Christ, God's Be-lov-ed, has come
found in the manger.

Found in the manger.
Grace born for humanity.
Be-lov-ed, You're loved!

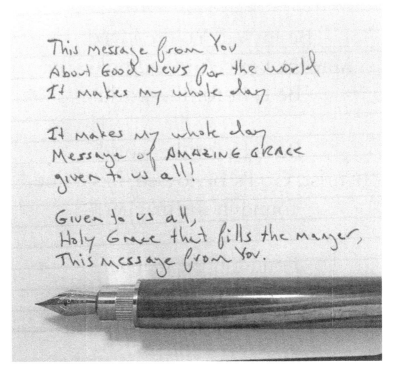

This message from You
About Good News for the world
It makes my whole day

It makes my whole day
Message of AMAZING GRACE
given to us all!

Given to us all,
Holy Grace that fills the manger,
This message from You.

This message from You,
about Good News for the world.
It makes my whole day.

It makes my whole day.
Message of Amazing Grace
given to us all!

Given to us all.
Holy Grace fills the manger.
This message from You.

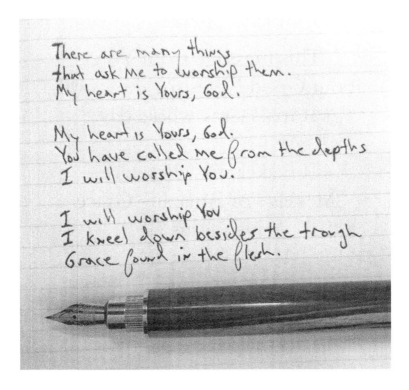

There are many things
that ask me to worship them.
My heart is Yours, God.

My heart is Yours, God.
You have called me from the depths
I will worship You.

I will worship You
I kneel down besides the trough
Grace found in the flesh.

There are many things
that ask me to worship them.
My heart is Yours, God.

My heart is Yours, God.
You have called me from the depths.
I will worship You.

I will worship You.
I kneel down besides the trough.
Grace found in the flesh.

Baptismal waters
Grace soaking into my soul
restoring me whole

Restoring me whole
Water healing my hurt heart
Work of the Spirit

Work of the Spirit
Amazing Grace found within
Baptismal waters.

Baptismal waters.
Grace soaking into my soul
restoring me whole.

Restoring me whole.
Water healing my hurt heart.
Work of the Spirit.

Work of the Spirit.
Amazing Grace found within
Baptismal waters.

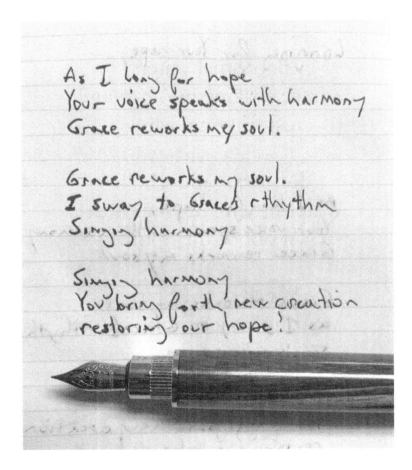

As I long for hope
Your voice speaks with harmony
Grace reworks my soul.

Grace reworks my soul.
I sway to Grace's rhythm
Singing harmony

Singing harmony
You bring forth new creation
restoring our hope!

As I long for hope.
Your voice speaks with harmony.
Grace reworks my soul.

Grace reworks my soul.
I sway to Grace's rhythm,
Singing harmony.

Singing harmony.
You bring forth new creation
restoring our hope!

Grace moves me closer
to the place that feels foreign:
The embrace of God.

The embrace of God
reminds me that I am loved
Because of God's Grace

Because of God's Grace
Found within this feeling trough,
Christ moves in closer.

Grace moves me closer
to the place that feel foreign.
The embrace of God.

The embrace of God
reminds me that I am loved
because of God's Grace.

Because of God's Grace,
Found within this feeding trough,
Christ moves in closer.

Root me in Your Grace.
You claim me again in Your
Baptismal waters

Baptismal waters
Rooted in the promise, God,
You won't let us go.

You won't let us go,
as Spirit born water bathes us.
Root us in Your Grace.

Root me in Your Grace.
You claim me again in Your
Baptismal waters.

Baptismal waters.
Rooted in the promise, God,
You won't let us go.

You won't let us go,
Spirit born water bathes us.
Root us in Your Grace.

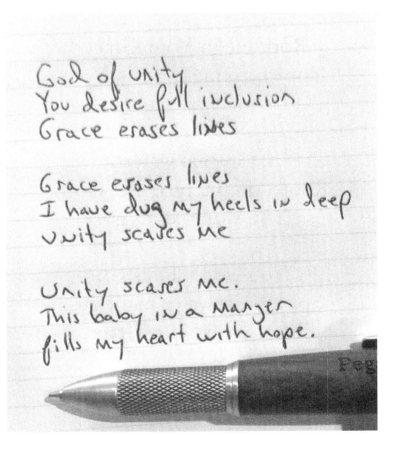

God of unity
You desire full inclusion
Grace erases lines

Grace erases lines
I have dug my heels in deep
Unity scares me

Unity scares me.
This baby in a manger
fills my heart with hope.

God of unity,
You desire full inclusion.
Grace erases lines.

Grace erases lines.
I have dug my heels in deep.
Unity scares me.

Unity scares me.
This baby in a manger
fills my heart with hope.

Unexpected Grace
Surprises me once again
erasing all lines

Unexpected Grace
tearing open the heavens
to find you and me

Unexpected Grace
Comes like a thief in the night
Stealing our sorrows

Unexpected Grace
surprises me once again,
erasing all lines.

Unexpected Grace
tearing open the heavens
to find you and me.

Unexpected Grace
comes like a thief in the night
stealing our sorrows.

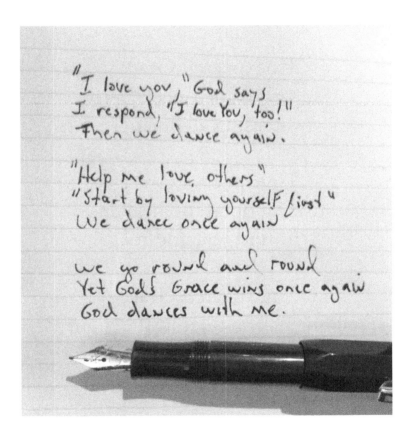

"I love you," God says
I respond, "I love You, too!"
Then we dance again.

"Help me love others"
"Start by loving yourself first"
We dance once again

we go round and round
Yet Gods Grace wins once again
God dances with me.

"I love you," God says.
I respond, "I love You, too!"
Then we dance again.

"Help me love others."
"Start by loving yourself first."
We dance once again.

We go round and round,
yet God's Grace wins once again.
God dances with me.

My heart is weighed down
with the worries of the world.
Please lighten my load.

Please lighten my load
teaching me to trust You, God.
Buoyancy of Grace

Buoyancy of Grace
counters the world's gravity
which has weighed me down.

My heart is weighed down
with the worries of the world.
Please lighten my load.

Please lighten my load,
teaching me to trust You, God.
Buoyancy of Grace.

Buoyancy of Grace
counters the world's gravity
which has weighed me down.

Change my heart, O'God
Help me act with Your mercy
Moving in with Grace

Moving in with Grace
The Stranger looks like Jesus
World paradigm shifts

World paradigm shift
as Grace erases our lives
Change my heart, O'God

Change my heart, O' God.
Help me act with Your mercy.
Moving in with Grace.

Moving in with Grace.
The Stranger looks like Jesus.
World paradigm shifts.

World paradigm shift
as Grace erases our lines.
Change my heart, O' God.

Jesus, Peace Bringer
Heart is restless and worried
I rest in Your Grace

I rest in Your Grace
Needing to open my heart
Dumping out my grief

Dumping out my grief,
the gift of Your Grace holds me
Jesus, Peace Bringer

Jesus, Peace Bringer.
Heart is restless and worried.
I rest in Your Grace.

I rest in Your Grace
needing to open my heart.
Dumping out my grief.

Dumping out my grief,
the gift of Your Grace holds me.
Jesus, Peace Bringer.

Worry takes over
Anxiety's drum beat leads.
Please punch my dance card.

Worry takes over
Anxiety wants to lead
Help me dance with You

Worry takes over
Fear lies and says I can't dance
Grace gives me rhythm.

Worry takes over.
Anxiety's drum beat leads.
Please punch my dance card.

Worry takes over.
Anxiety wants to lead.
Help me dance with You.

Worry takes over.
Fear lies and says I can't dance.
Grace gives me rhythm.

Feet washed; Dinner served
Peter and Judas both eat
Grace washes their toes

Grace washes their toes
One denies; one hands over
Jesus washes both

Jesus washes both
Jesus feeds us the same meal
Feet washed; Dinner served

Feet washed; dinner served.
Peter and Judas both eat.
Grace washes their toes.

Grace washes their toes.
One denies; one hands over.
Jesus washes both.

Jesus washes both.
Jesus feeds us the same meal.
Feet washed; dinner served.

Gracious Advocate
I need You more than ever
Please enter my heart

Please enter my heart
Find the cracks in my armor
Grace needs a way in

Grace needs a way in
I trust You are here to heal
Gracious Advocate

Gracious Advocate.
I need You more than ever.
Please enter my heart.

Please enter my heart.
Find the cracks in my armor.
Grace needs a way in.

Grace needs a way in.
I trust You are here to heal.
Gracious Advocate.

In the dark of night
My soul hurts and so I cry
I long for Your Grace

I long for Your Grace
I cry out, "How long O'God?"
Tears baptize the Ground

Tears baptize the Ground
I cry inside as tears flow
Grace envelops me.

In the dark of night,
My soul hurts and so I cry.
I long for Your Grace.

I long for Your Grace.
I cry out, "How long O' God?"
Tears baptize the ground.

Tears baptize the ground.
I cry inside as tears flow.
Grace envelops me.

As I close my eyes,
worries play like a movie.
Please help me rest, God.

Please help me rest God
Stories of my failings told.
I need a rewrite.

I need a rewrite
The title is, "Grace Abounds!"
where I rest assured.

As I close my eyes,
worries play like a movie.
Please help me rest, God.

Please help me rest, God.
Stories of my failings told.
I need a rewrite.

I need a rewrite.
The title is, "Grace Abounds!"
where I rest assured.

Repent. Turn Around.
This word is without judgement
My heart still feels pain.

My heart still feels pain.
My need to repent is clear.
God, I need Your Grace.

God, I need Your Grace.
Help me see love in the words:
Repent. Turn Around.

Repent. Turn around.
This word is without judgment.
My heart still feels pain.

My heart still feels pain.
My need to repent is clear.
God, I need Your Grace.

God, I need Your Grace.
Help me see love in the words:
Repent. Turn around.

You have amazed me
Stone rolled away; my heart opened
Jesus is Risen!

Jesus is Risen!
Yes, He is Risen, Indeed!
I'm amazed by Grace

I'm amazed by Grace
This new resurrected life
God has gifted me!

You have amazed me.
Stone rolled away; heart opened.
Jesus is risen!

Jesus is risen!
Yes, He is risen, indeed!
I'm amazed by Grace.

I'm amazed by Grace.
This new resurrected life
God has gifted me!

ABOUT THE AUTHOR

John W. Stevens is an ordained pastor in the Evangelical Lutheran Church in America, and currently serves Zion Lutheran, located in Oregon City, Oregon.

When John isn't writing Haiku, or other styles of poetry, he can be found roasting coffee, creating children's sermon springboards, or practicing sleight of hand magic. John has also been seen casting a fishing line into a lake in the Pioneer Mountains of Montana in hopes of catching trout.

John lives in Camas, Washington, and more than anything else, loves to spend time with his family.

Made in the USA
Coppell, TX
29 September 2023

22165037R00174